ANNE WILLAN

Bistro

ANNE WILLAN

Bistro

Photography by Philip Wilkins

WEIDENFELD & NICOLSON

Anne Willan

Anne Willan has more than 30 years experience as a teacher, cookbook author and food columnist. She has written many books, including the influential *Reader's Digest Complete Guide to Cookery* and the 17-volume *Look and Cook* series, which also featured on television in Britain and the USA.

Anne Willan founded Ecole de Cuisine La Varenne in Paris in 1975 and continues to direct its culinary programs at the Château du Feÿ in Burgundy and at The Greenbrier in West Virginia. She has served as the President of the International Association of Culinary Professionals and has just completed her next major work, *Cooked to Perfection*, to be published in autumn 1997.

Contents

POTAGE DE POTIRON ET POIREAUX 10
PUMPKIN AND LEEK SOUP

FRISÉE AUX LARDONS 12
SALAD OF CURLY ENDIVE WITH HOT BACON DRESSING

CHAUDRÉE DE MOULES AU FENOUIL ET SAFRAN 14
COD AND MUSSEL CHOWDER WITH FENNEL AND SAFFRON

SAUMON À LA PEAU CROUSTILLANTE, COULIS DE TOMATES ET BASILIC 16
CRISP-SKINNED SALMON FILLET, TOMATO AND BASIL COULIS

POULET EN COCOTTE AUX QUARANTE GOUSSES D'AIL 18
POT-ROAST CHICKEN WITH FORTY GARLIC CLOVES

POT-AU-FEU À L'ANCIENNE 20

LAPIN AUX PRUNEAUX 22
RABBIT WITH PRUNES

POMMES DE TERRE ÉCRASÉES AUX OLIVES NOIRES 24
CRUSHED POTATOES WITH BLACK OLIVES

LA VRAIE RATATOUILLE 26
REAL RATATOUILLE

POUDING DE RIZ CARAMELISÉ AUX RAISINS MACÉRÉS 28
CARAMELIZED RICE PUDDING WITH TIPSY RAISINS

TARTE AUX POIRES NORMANDE 30
PEAR AND ALMOND TART

LA MOUSSE AU CHOCOLAT DE CHEF CHAMBRETTE 32
CHEF CHAMBRETTE'S CHOCOLATE MOUSSE

THE BASICS

    CHICKEN STOCK 34

    VEAL STOCK 34

    BOUQUET GARNI 35

    TO CLEAN MUSSELS 35

    TO SKIN, SEED AND CHOP TOMATOES 35

    TO CUT UP A RABBIT 36

    TO MAKE CRÈME FRAÎCHE 36

    PIE PASTRY 37

    TO LINE A TART TIN 37

An apple pie
without the cheese
is like a kiss
without the squeeze.

YORKSHIRE ADAGE

Introduction

Mention the word bistro and the atmosphere lightens at once. Faces relax as chefs reach for their favourite heavy copper pots and battered black casseroles. Warming aromas, generous portions, dishes that grandmother made, all are part of the bistro image. Like so much good cooking, the bistro style began in France. Although it has spread worldwide, we still associate a good bistro with French favourites such as poulet en cocotte, pot-au-feu or mousse au chocolat, dishes we all find easy to love.

Bistro cooking has not stood still. Recently a whole new repertoire has evolved of lighter dishes, making generous use of fish, vegetables and salads. Asian ingredients appear, and quicker methods of cooking than the time-honoured simmering of soups and ragoûts. Desserts may have the name pudding or pie, but they will be fluffy with egg whites, pastry will be wafer-thin, and the emphasis will be on healthy fruits, on sorbets and soufflés. But the inspiration remains the same: a cuisine that draws heavily on the past but flourishes in the present, easy on the pocket, welcoming on the plate and second to none on the palate. I hardly need to add, bon appétit!

POTAGE DE POTIRON ET POIREAUX

1 kg/2¼ lb pumpkin
1 potato, quartered
4 leeks, about 500 g/1 lb 2 oz
1.2 litres/2 pints water
large pinch of ground nutmeg
salt and pepper
125 ml/4 fl oz crème fraîche or
   double cream
pinch of sugar (optional)
25 g/1 oz butter, cut into pieces
1–2 tablespoons chopped fresh
   chives

Peel the pumpkin and discard the seeds and tough fibres. Cut the flesh into pieces the same size as the potato. Halve the leeks lengthways, slice the white and pale green parts into 2.5 cm/1 inch pieces and rinse in a colander to wash away the grit.

Put the pumpkin, potato, leeks and water in a large saucepan with the nutmeg, salt and pepper. Cover, bring to the boil and simmer until the vegetables are very tender, about 30 minutes.

Strain the liquid into a large jug and reserve. Work the vegetables through a sieve or food mill back into the saucepan, discarding the fibres from the sieve. Stir in the reserved liquid.

Shortly before serving, reheat the soup in the pan with half the cream, adding more water if the soup is very thick. Taste and adjust the seasoning, adding sugar and more nutmeg if it seems bland. Remove the soup from the heat, add the butter pieces and stir until melted. Spoon into warmed bowls, stir a spoonful of the remaining cream into each bowl and top with a sprinkling of chives.

Butternut squash can be substituted for the pumpkin, onions for the leeks. For an autumnal approach, leave out all but one leek and add an 800 g/1¾ lb can of cooked whole chestnuts in water, drained, just before serving.

Pumpkin soup is perfect before a roast bird – turkey, chicken or game such as pheasant. Baste the bird with butter and make generous amounts of wine gravy. For dessert? Chocolate crème brûlée or vanilla ice cream with chocolate sauce and a sprinkling of toasted hazelnuts would be my choice.

Frisée aux lardons

**SERVES 4 AS A FIRST COURSE,
2 AS A MAIN COURSE**

a large head (about 450 g/1 lb)
   curly endive or escarole
1 tablespoon vegetable oil
175 g/6 oz thickly sliced lean
   smoked bacon, diced
2 garlic cloves, thinly sliced
5 tablespoons red wine vinegar
freshly ground black pepper

Discard the tough outer green leaves from the curly
endive or escarole and pull apart the central white
leaves. Wash, dry well and put them in a salad bowl.

Just before serving, heat the oil in a frying pan, add the
bacon and fry, stirring often. When the bacon is well
browned and the fat is rendered, lower the heat and
discard some fat if you have more than 3–4 tablespoons.
Add the garlic and cook until the garlic is soft and
fragrant but not browned, about 30 seconds. Pour the
hot fat, bacon and garlic over the leaves and toss
thoroughly so they wilt slightly.

Return the pan to the heat, add the vinegar and boil for
a few seconds, until reduced by half, stirring to dissolve
the pan juices. Pour them over the salad and toss again.
Add pepper to taste and spoon the salad on to warmed
individual plates or bowls. Serve at once.

Fried croûtons, walnuts or a poached egg are optional
additions.

*This salad is the classic start to a winter meal. For a main
course, look no further than coq au vin, boeuf bourguignon or
blanquette de veau, with fresh noodles or boiled rice. I would
add a traditional dessert such as floating island, crème caramel
or chocolate mousse to finish a nostalgic menu which is right
back in style.*

CHAUDRÉE DE MOULES AU FENOUIL ET SAFRAN

SERVES 4

25 g/1 oz butter
325 g/12 oz fennel bulb, sliced
1 onion, chopped
salt and white pepper
800 g/1¾ lb potatoes, peeled
　and cut into 2.5 cm/1 inch
　cubes
large pinch of saffron threads
250 ml/8 fl oz fish stock
1 bay leaf
800 g/1¾ lb mussels
500 g/1 lb 2 oz cod fillets,
　skinned and cut into
　2.5 cm/1 inch pieces
500 ml/16 fl oz milk
250 ml/8 fl oz double cream
2 tablespoons chopped fresh
　parsley

Melt the butter in a saucepan and add the fennel, onion, salt and pepper. Sauté gently, stirring occasionally, until the vegetables are translucent but not starting to brown, 7–10 minutes.

Spread the potatoes over the fennel. Mix the saffron with the fish stock and pour it over the potatoes. Add the bay leaf, cover and bring to the boil, then reduce the heat and simmer until the potatoes are just tender, 12–15 minutes.

Meanwhile, clean the mussels thoroughly (page 35).

Spread the cod over the potatoes and add the milk. Stir to mix the ingredients and spread the colour of the saffron. Add the mussels, cover tightly with the lid and simmer until the fish is just tender when flaked with a fork and the mussels have opened, 5–7 minutes. Note that the milk should simmer, not boil, or it may curdle.

Add the cream and parsley and bring just to the boil. Discard the bay leaf, taste and adjust the seasoning. Serve the chowder from the casserole, or in individual bowls.

This fish chowder is not a soup but a stew, a generous meal in itself. Serve it with sliced baguette, baked in the oven until dry so it forms croûtes for soaking in the stew. A good dessert would be figs baked in port wine or poached pears with candied ginger.

SAUMON À LA PEAU CROUSTILLANTE, COULIS DE TOMATES ET BASILIC

SERVES 4

1–2 salmon fillets, scaled, with skin, about 800 g/1¾ lb
salt and pepper
2 tablespoons olive oil

Tomato and basil coulis
500 g/1 lb 2 oz tomatoes, skinned, seeded and diced
bunch of basil
1 garlic clove, finely chopped
juice of 1 lemon, or more to taste

To make the coulis: sprinkle the diced tomatoes with salt and pepper, stir gently and leave to drain in a colander for 15–30 minutes. Strip the basil leaves from the stems, reserving several sprigs for decoration. Shred the remaining leaves. Put the drained tomatoes in a bowl and stir in the garlic, lemon juice and shredded basil. Taste, adjust the seasoning and chill the coulis.

Preheat the oven to 220°C/425°F/Gas Mark 7. To prepare the salmon: run your fingers over the flesh and if you feel any bones, pull them out with tweezers. Cut the salmon into four portions and sprinkle both sides with salt and pepper. Heat the oil in a large frying pan with an ovenproof handle and add the salmon, skin side down. Fry without moving the pieces for 2–3 minutes, until the skin is crisp – when done it will shrink and loosen from the surface of the pan. Transfer the pan to the oven and bake until done to your taste: 2–4 minutes for rare, 5–8 minutes for well done. Note that cooking time depends on the thickness of the fish.

Transfer the fish to warmed serving plates, skin side up. Stir the coulis to blend, taste it again, adjusting the seasoning if necessary. Spoon the chilled coulis beside the hot fish, decorate the plates with basil sprigs and serve at once so the skin remains crisp.

Keep this salmon up to speed with an accompaniment of couscous flavoured with saffron. For dessert, I'd go for an open face fruit tart, the pastry rolled wafer-thin in the modern style.

POULET EN COCOTTE AUX QUARANTE GOUSSES D'AIL

SERVES 4

3–4 whole heads of garlic*
1 chicken, about 1.8 kg/4 lb
salt and pepper
4–5 sprigs of thyme
25 g/1 oz butter
about 500 ml/16 fl oz chicken
   stock

*You'll need fewer cloves in
winter, when garlic is drier
and more pungent.

Preheat the oven to 190°C/375°F/Gas Mark 5. Separate the garlic heads into cloves, leaving them unpeeled. Season the chicken inside and out with salt and pepper, add 2–3 sprigs of thyme to the cavity and truss the bird.

Heat the butter in a casserole, add the chicken and brown over medium heat, turning so it colours evenly on all sides, 8–10 minutes. Add the garlic cloves, the remaining thyme, and enough stock to cover completely. Cover and cook in the oven until very tender, 50–60 minutes; test by piercing the thigh with a two-pronged fork. The meat will start to shrink from the drumstick bones and the garlic cloves will be very soft. Check from time to time during cooking and if the chicken seems dry, add more stock.

Transfer the chicken and half the garlic cloves to a serving dish, cover and keep warm. Work the remaining garlic with the cooking liquid through a strainer into a small saucepan, pressing well to extract all the garlic pulp and form a sauce. Bring to the boil. If necessary, simmer to reduce it until slightly thickened. Taste the sauce and adjust the seasoning. Discard the trussing strings from the chicken (but leave the garlic unpeeled for guests to squeeze out the soft pulp) and serve the sauce in a separate bowl.

This is good with roasted or glazed root vegetables – turnips, carrots, celeriac, beetroot and potatoes. Alternatively, simply toast slices of country bread to act as background to the garlic purée. In summer I would start the meal with a fresh tomato salad, in winter with a tomato soup. For dessert a batter pudding (clafoutis) of seasonal fruit such as cherries, apricots, apples or dried prunes would be an appropriate finish.

POT-AU-FEU À L'ANCIENNE

SERVES 8

1.5 kg/3 lb piece of beef or veal
shank, with bone
1 kg/2¼ lb piece of beef chuck
or brisket
1 kg/2¼ lb beef short ribs
1 onion, studded with 4 cloves
large bouquet garni
salt
1 tablespoon black peppercorns
1 stick of celery
1 cinnamon stick
8 beef marrow bones
1 kg/2¼ lb carrots,
quartered and cut into
8 cm/3 inch sticks
1.5 kg/3 lb leeks, trimmed,
halved lengthways and cut
into 8 cm/3 inch sticks
675 g/1½ lb turnips, cut
into eighths
125 g/4 oz angel hair pasta

To serve
sea salt
gherkin pickles
mustard

Note: cooking takes a day
from start to finish, and I like
to start 2 days ahead so the
flavours mellow.

Put all the meat into a large stockpot with enough water to cover generously. Bring slowly to the boil, skimming often. Add the onion, bouquet garni, salt, peppercorns, celery and cinnamon stick. Tie each marrow bone in muslin and add to the pot. Simmer very gently, uncovered, skimming occasionally, for 3 hours.

Wrap the carrots, leeks and turnips in separate bundles in muslin. Add to the pot, pushing them down into the broth and adding more water if needed to cover them. Simmer for another hour or until the meats and vegetables are very tender. If some are done before others, remove them. Be sure there is always enough broth to cover the meats and vegetables during cooking.

Transfer the bones, meats and vegetables to a board. Strain the broth into a clean saucepan, then boil it until reduced by half, or until well flavoured. Taste and adjust the seasoning. If preparing ahead, replace the meats and vegetables in the broth and refrigerate. (Reheat all in the broth.)

Unwrap the bones and arrange them on a very large platter. Slice the meats and arrange them overlapping on the platter. Unwrap the vegetables and pile them in mounds on the platter. Cover it with foil and keep warm.

For the first course, add the pasta to the reduced broth and simmer for 3–5 minutes. Taste the broth and adjust the seasoning, then transfer to a tureen and serve.

For the main course, serve the platter of meats and vegetables with sea salt, gherkins and mustard.

Don't let dessert be an anticlimax – serve your very best fruit pie.

LAPIN AUX PRUNEAUX

SERVES 4

1 rabbit, about 1.8 kg/4 lb*
175 g/6 oz pitted prunes
1 tablespoon vegetable oil
1 tablespoon butter
1 tablespoon plain flour
250 ml/8 fl oz red wine
375 ml/12 fl oz veal
    or chicken stock
1 garlic clove, chopped
salt and pepper
1 tablespoon chopped
    fresh parsley

Marinade
500 ml/16 fl oz red wine
large bouquet garni
1 onion, chopped
1 carrot, chopped
1 teaspoon crushed black
    peppercorns
1 tablespoon vegetable oil

*Or 1 large chicken, cut into
eight pieces.

Cut the rabbit into six or seven pieces (page 36). Stir all the marinade ingredients except the oil together in a deep, non-metallic bowl. Add the pieces of rabbit, pushing them down into the liquid. Spoon over the oil, cover and refrigerate for 1–2 days.

Pour boiling water over the prunes to cover and leave to soak. Remove the rabbit from the marinade and pat dry. Strain the marinade into a jug and reserve the liquid and the vegetables.

Heat the oil and butter in a sauté pan or shallow flame-proof casserole and brown the rabbit pieces on all sides, 5–7 minutes. Remove the rabbit, add the onion and carrot from the marinade and sauté until starting to brown, 5–7 minutes. Stir in the flour and continue cooking, stirring constantly, until well browned. Stir in the reserved marinade and the red wine and bring to the boil. Add the stock, garlic, any liquid from the prunes, the bouquet garni, salt and pepper. Replace the rabbit pieces, cover and simmer for 30 minutes.

Add the prunes and continue simmering – removing the lid if the sauce is thin and needs reducing – until the rabbit is very tender. Transfer the rabbit to a serving dish, spoon the prunes on top, cover and keep warm. If necessary, boil the sauce to reduce until it just coats a spoon. Discard the bouquet garni, taste the sauce and adjust the seasoning. Spoon the sauce over the rabbit, sprinkle with parsley and serve.

Rabbit with prunes just asks for the comfort of potato purée and a dish of glazed carrots or turnips. Begin with a soup of peppery greens such as watercress or spinach, and end with a caramelized rice pudding (page 28).

POMMES DE TERRE ÉCRASÉES AUX OLIVES NOIRES

SERVES 4

675 g/1½ lb potatoes, unpeeled
salt and pepper
150 g/5 oz black olives
125 ml/4 fl oz extra virgin
    olive oil

Cut each potato into two or three pieces and put them into a saucepan of cold salted water. Cover, bring to the boil and simmer until the potatoes are very tender when pierced with the point of a knife, 15−20 minutes. Meanwhile, pit and coarsely shred the olives.

Drain the potatoes, leave to cool slightly, then peel them. Return them to the pan and heat gently for 4−5 minutes to evaporate any moisture. Crush them with a potato masher or a fork. Using the masher or fork, stir in the olives, olive oil and pepper. Do not overmix. Taste and adjust the seasoning, adding more oil if you wish.

When a recipe uses only three ingredients, it's clear that their quality is all-important. King Edward, Romano, Pentland Dell or Pentland Squire make good, fluffy mash. I use oil-cured black olives, full-flavoured but not salty − be sure to taste them first.

These potatoes are very Mediterranean in style, wonderful with grilled fish or roast duck and a salad of rocket or sweet roasted red peppers. Continuing with pungent flavours, for dessert what could be better than lemon tart or a salad of fresh oranges topped with crisp caramel?

LA VRAIE RATATOUILLE

SERVES 4–6

2 small aubergines, about 400 g/14 oz
3 small courgettes, about 400 g/14 oz
salt and pepper
150 ml/5 fl oz olive oil
2 onions, sliced
2 red peppers, cored, seeded and sliced
2 green peppers, cored, seeded and sliced
800 g/1¾ lb plum tomatoes, skinned, seeded and chopped
4 garlic cloves, chopped
1 tablespoon coriander seeds
1 teaspoon fennel seeds
4–5 sprigs of thyme
2–3 sprigs of rosemary
2 bay leaves

Note: ratatouille should be made at least a day ahead so the flavours have time to develop.

Trim the ends of the aubergines and courgettes without peeling them. Cut the aubergines into 2 cm/¾ inch cubes. Halve the courgettes lengthways and then cut them into 1 cm/½ inch slices.

Put the aubergines and courgettes into a colander, sprinkle generously with salt and toss to mix. Leave for 30 minutes to draw out the juices. Rinse well and drain on paper towels.

Heat 2–3 tablespoons of the oil in a heavy casserole, add the onions and fry until soft, 3–5 minutes. Add the aubergines and courgettes, peppers, tomatoes, garlic, coriander and fennel seeds, salt, pepper and remaining oil and heat, stirring, until very hot. Tie the thyme, rosemary and bay leaves into two or three bundles with string and add to the casserole. Cover and cook over low heat for 30–40 minutes, until the vegetables are very tender and any liquid is reduced and concentrated. Stir often, particularly towards the end of cooking, and if necessary remove the lid so that the liquid evaporates.

Discard the herb bundles, taste the ratatouille and adjust the seasoning. Let it cool and store overnight in the refrigerator. For maximum flavour, serve at room temperature and check the seasoning just before serving.

Ratatouille is wonderfully versatile. It can act as a first course or an accompaniment to roast chicken, lamb, beef or even grilled fish. I've served it over spaghetti with great success, topped with a sprinkling of Parmesan cheese. Dessert can be minimal – perhaps some chilled slices of melon, or strawberries or raspberries sprinkled with a little sugar and balsamic vinegar to draw out their juice.

POUDING DE RIZ CARAMELISÉ AUX RAISINS MACÉRÉS

SERVES 4

3 tablespoons raisins
2 tablespoons rum
1 litre/1¾ pints milk,
  or more if needed
100 g/3½ oz round-grain rice
1 vanilla bean, split
pinch of salt
3 tablespoons sugar, or to taste
2 eggs

Caramel
100 g/3½ oz sugar
5 tablespoons cold water

To serve
125 ml/4 fl oz double cream

Note: I find the flavour improves
if the puddings are chilled for
1–2 days.

Put the raisins and rum in a saucepan, heat until quite hot, then remove from the heat and leave to macerate.

Bring the milk to the boil in a heavy saucepan and stir in the rice, vanilla bean and salt. Simmer, uncovered, stirring occasionally, until the rice is very tender, 30–40 minutes. If necessary add more milk during cooking – when done the milk should just be absorbed.

Meanwhile, make the caramel. Heat the sugar and water in a heavy saucepan until the sugar dissolves. Bring to the boil and boil steadily without stirring until the syrup starts to colour. Lower the heat and boil until the syrup cooks to a dark caramel. Remove from the heat, let the bubbles subside and then pour the caramel into four ramekins: beware, it is very hot. Leave to set.

Preheat the oven to 180°C/350°F/Gas Mark 4. When the rice is cooked, remove the vanilla bean, stir in the raisins, rum and sugar and taste, adding more sugar if needed. Whisk the eggs until pale and stir them into the rice. Spoon the rice into the caramel-lined ramekins.

Set the ramekins in a roasting pan of hot water and bring to the boil on top of the stove. Transfer it to the oven and bake until the puddings are just set, 20–25 minutes. Remove them from the water bath and leave until cold.

To serve, run a knife around the edge of each pudding and turn out on to plates. Spoon cream around them.

Roast meat, for me, is the right partner for rice pudding. In France the beef would probably come with little fried potatoes and baked tomatoes topped with garlic, parsley and breadcrumbs à la Provençale, or the lamb with green beans or flageolet beans.

TARTE AUX POIRES NORMANDE

SERVES 6-8

pie pastry (page 37)
3–4 ripe pears, about
  600 g/1¼ lb
caster sugar for sprinkling

Almond frangipane
100 g/3½ oz unsalted butter
100 g/3½ oz caster sugar
1 egg
1 egg yolk
1 tablespoon Calvados
  or Cognac
100 g/3½ oz ground blanched
  almonds
2 tablespoons plain flour

Roll out the chilled pastry, line a 25 cm/10 inch tart tin with a removable base and chill until firm, 15–30 minutes. Preheat the oven to 200°C/400°F/Gas Mark 6 and place a baking sheet in the lower third of the oven.

For the frangipane: cream the butter, gradually beat in the sugar and continue beating until the mixture is soft and light, 2–3 minutes. Beat in the egg and egg yolk. Add the Calvados or Cognac, then stir in the ground almonds and flour. Spread the frangipane in the chilled pastry shell.

Peel the pears, halve them, and scoop out the cores. Set the halves flat on a board and cut across into very thin slices, retaining the pear shape. Flatten them slightly to elongate the pear shape, then lift with a palette knife and carefully place on the frangipane.

Set the tart on the heated baking sheet and bake until the pastry starts to brown, 10–15 minutes. Lower the heat to 180°C/350°F/Gas Mark 4 and continue baking for 10–15 minutes. Sprinkle the tart with sugar and bake for a further 10 minutes, until the pears are tender, the frangipane is set and the sugar is slightly caramelized. The tart will shrink from the sides of the tin.

Leave the tart on a wire rack to cool for 5 minutes, then remove the sides of the tart tin. Let the tart cool to tepid before removing the base. Serve at room temperature.

Pears are an autumn fruit, the seasonal partner of goose, turkey or game simmered with red wine and onions as a dark ragoût. To accompany the ragoût I would turn to braised red cabbage, with a purée of chestnuts or celeriac. Cheese must come somewhere in the meal, perhaps toasted on croûtes to serve with salad.

LA MOUSSE AU CHOCOLAT DE CHEF CHAMBRETTE

SERVES 4–6

175 g/6 oz good-quality plain
  chocolate, chopped
250 ml/8 fl oz fresh orange juice
2 tablespoons Grand Marnier
4 egg whites
25 g/1 oz caster sugar
cocoa powder for sprinkling

Candied zest

pared zest of 1 orange
2 tablespoons sugar
2 tablespoons water

In a heavy saucepan melt the chocolate in the orange juice, stirring gently. Bring to the boil and simmer for 3–4 minutes, stirring constantly until it has the consistency of double cream. Let it cool to tepid, then stir in the Grand Marnier.

Whisk the egg whites until stiff. Add the sugar and continue beating until glossy, about 30 seconds. Stir about a quarter of the whites into the chocolate until well mixed and light. Add this mixture back into the remaining whites and fold together as lightly as possible. Spoon the mousse into small pots or ramekins and tap them on the work surface to level the mixture. Cover and chill until set – at least 6 and up to 24 hours.

Not more than 1 hour before serving, candy the zest: cut the orange zest into the finest possible julienne strips. In a small saucepan heat the sugar and water until dissolved. Add the orange strips and simmer very gently, stirring occasionally, until the zests are translucent and the syrup has evaporated, 7–10 minutes. Spread the zests on a sheet of greaseproof paper and leave to dry for 15–30 minutes.

Just before serving, sprinkle the mousses with cocoa and top each with a pinch of candied zest. Serve chilled.

I was given this recipe by Chef Fernand Chambrette, who in the long-ago 1950s was awarded two Michelin stars for his mastery of bistro dishes such as duck confit and rum babas. He liked to melt the chocolate in strong black coffee; here I use orange juice. Chef Chambrette was famous for his hand with fish. To precede this chocolate mousse I'm opting for grilled fillets of sole or John Dory with a tarragon butter sauce, asparagus on the side, and as opener a classic onion soup.

The Basics

CHICKEN STOCK

MAKES ABOUT 2.5 LITRES/4½ PINTS

1.5 kg/3 lb chicken backs, necks
    and bones
1 onion, quartered
1 carrot, quartered
1 stick of celery, chopped
bouquet garni
1 teaspoon peppercorns

Put all the ingredients into a large saucepan with about 4 litres/6½ pints water. Bring slowly to the boil, skimming often. Simmer uncovered for 2−3 hours, skimming occasionally.

Strain the stock, taste, and if the flavour is not concentrated, boil it until well reduced. Leave to cool, then refrigerate it. Before using, lift any solidified fat from the surface. Stock can be kept for up to 3 days in the refrigerator, or frozen.

VEAL STOCK

MAKES ABOUT 2.5 LITRES/4½ PINTS

2.2 kg/5 lb veal bones
2 onions, quartered
2 carrots, quartered
bouquet garni
1 teaspoon peppercorns
1 tablespoon tomato purée

Put the veal bones in a roasting tin and roast in a very hot oven, 230°C/450°F/Gas Mark 8, for 20 minutes. Add the onions and carrots and continue roasting until very brown, about 30 minutes longer. Transfer the bones and vegetables to a large saucepan or stockpot, discarding any fat. Add the bouquet garni, peppercorns, tomato purée and about 5 litres/9 pints water. Bring slowly to the boil, then simmer uncovered for 4−5 hours, skimming occasionally.

Strain the stock, taste and, if the flavour is not concentrated, boil it until well reduced. Leave to cool, then refrigerate it. Before using, lift any solidified fat from the surface. Stock can be kept for up to 3 days in the refrigerator, or frozen.

BOUQUET GARNI

A bundle of aromatic herbs used for flavouring stocks, braises and ragoûts. It should include a generous sprig of thyme, a bay leaf and several sprigs of parsley or parsley stalks, tied together with string. A piece of green leek and/or some celery tops may also be included.

TO CLEAN MUSSELS

Wash the mussels under cold running water, scraping the shells clean with a knife and removing any weeds. Discard any mussels with broken shells and any that do not close when tapped because this indicates that the mussel may be dead. The 'beard', or tough seaweed-like thread dangling from inside the shell, should be removed only just before cooking the mussels.

TO SKIN, SEED AND CHOP TOMATOES

Pull off the tomato stalks and mark a small cross at the opposite end with the tip of a knife. Put the tomatoes in a small bowl, pour boiling water over them and leave for 10 seconds or until the skin starts to curl away at the cross. Drain and peel them. Halve them crossways like a grapefruit and squeeze to remove the seeds. The seeds can be rubbed in a sieve to extract the juice. Cut the tomato halves in slices, then chop them.

TO CUT UP A RABBIT

Trim and discard the flaps of skin, tips of forelegs and any excess bone. Using a heavy knife or cleaver, divide the rabbit crossways into three sections: back legs, back, and forelegs including the rib cage. Cut between the back legs to separate them; trim the end of the backbone. Chop the front of the rabbit in half to separate the forelegs. Cut the back crossways into two or three pieces depending on the size, giving six or seven pieces. Leave the kidneys (if present) attached to the ribs.

TO MAKE CRÈME FRAÎCHE

This French cream has a slightly tart flavour which is particularly good in sauces and stews. To make 750 ml/ 1¼ pints of crème fraîche, stir together in a saucepan 500 ml/16 fl oz of double cream, 250 ml/8 fl oz buttermilk and the juice of ½ lemon. Heat gently until just below body temperature, 25°C/75°F. Pour the cream into a container and partly cover it. Keep it at this temperature for 5–8 hours or until it has thickened and tastes slightly acid. The cream will thicken faster on a hot day. Stir it and store it in the refrigerator; it will keep for up to 2 weeks.

PIE PASTRY

200 g/7 oz flour
100 g/3½ oz unsalted butter
1 egg yolk
½ teaspoon salt

Sift the flour on to a work surface and make a well in the centre. Pound the butter with your fist to soften it slightly. Add the butter, egg yolk, salt and 3 tablespoons cold water to the well and work with your fingertips until mixed. Using a pastry scraper or metal spatula, draw in the flour and work until coarse crumbs are formed. If crumbs seem dry, add 1–2 tablespoons more water. Gently press the dough into a ball; it should be soft but not sticky.

Lightly flour the work surface and blend the dough by pushing it away with the heel of your hand and gathering it up with a scraper. After 1–2 minutes the dough should be smooth and peel easily from the work surface. Press it into a ball, wrap in greaseproof paper and chill for 30 minutes.

TO LINE A TART TIN WITH PASTRY

Butter the tin. On a lightly floured surface, roll out the pastry to 5 mm/¼ inch thick. Wrap the pastry around the rolling pin, lift it over the tin and unroll it. Let the pastry rest over the edge of the tin, overlapping it slightly inside. Be careful not to stretch the pastry. Gently lift the edges of the pastry with one hand and press it well into the bottom corners of the tin with the other.

Roll the rolling pin over the top of the tin to cut off the excess pastry. Using your forefinger and thumb, press the pastry evenly up the sides from the bottom to increase the height of the rim. Neaten the rim with your finger and thumb and flute it if you like. Do not let the pastry overlap the edge of the tin. Prick the base of the pastry so air bubbles do not form during cooking.

Classic Cooking

STARTERS
Lesley Waters A former chef and now a popular television cook, appearing regularly on *Ready Steady Cook* and *Can't Cook Won't Cook*. Author of several cookery books.

VEGETABLE SOUPS
Elisabeth Luard Cookery writer for the *Sunday Telegraph Magazine* and author of *European Peasant Food* and *European Festival Food*, which won a Glenfiddich Award.

GOURMET SALADS
Sonia Stevenson The first woman chef in the UK to be awarded a Michelin star, at the Horn of Plenty in Devon. Author of *The Magic of Saucery* and *Fresh Ways with Fish*.

FISH AND SHELLFISH
Gordon Ramsay Chef/proprietor of London's Aubergine restaurant, recently awarded its second Michelin star, and author of *A Passion for Flavour*.

CHICKEN, DUCK AND GAME
Nick Nairn Chef/patron of Braeval restaurant near Aberfoyle in Scotland, whose BBC-TV series *Wild Harvest* was last summer's most successful cookery series, accompanied by a book.

LIVERS, SWEETBREADS AND KIDNEYS
Simon Hopkinson Former chef/patron at London's Bibendum restaurant, columnist and author of *Roast Chicken and Other Stories* and *The Prawn Cocktail Years*.

VEGETARIAN
Rosamond Richardson Author of several vegetarian titles, including *The Great Green Cookbook* and *Food from Green Places*.

PASTA
Joy Davies One of the creators of *BBC Good Food Magazine*, she has been food editor of *She, Woman* and *Options* and written for the *Guardian, Daily Telegraph* and *Harpers & Queen*.

CHEESE DISHES
Rose Elliot The UK's most successful vegetarian cookery writer and author of many books, including *Not Just a Load of Old Lentils* and *The Classic Vegetarian Cookbook*.

POTATO DISHES
Patrick McDonald Former chef/patron of the acclaimed Epicurean restaurant in Cheltenham, and food consultant to Sir Rocco Forte Hotels.

BISTRO
Anne Willan Founder and director of La Varenne Cookery School in Burgundy and West Virginia. Author of many books and a specialist in French cuisine.

ITALIAN
Anna Del Conte Author of several books on Italian food, including *The Gastronomy of Italy, Secrets from an Italian Kitchen* and *The Classic Food of Northern Italy* (chosen as the 1996 Guild of Food Writers Book of the Year).

VIETNAMESE
Nicole Routhier One of the United States' most popular cookery writers, her books include *Cooking Under Wraps, Nicole Routhier's Fruit Cookbook* and the award-winning *The Foods of Vietnam*.

MALAYSIAN
Jill Dupleix One of Australia's best known cookery writers and broadcasters, with columns in the *Sydney Morning Herald* and *Elle*. Her books include *New Food* and *Allegro al dente*.

PEKING CUISINE
Helen Chen Author of *Chinese Home Cooking,* she learned to cook traditional Peking dishes from her mother, Joyce Chen, the *grande dame* of Chinese cooking in the United States.

STIR-FRIES
Kay Fairfax A writer and broadcaster whose books include *100 Great Stir-fries, Homemade* and *The Australian Christmas Book*.

NOODLES
Terry Durack Australia's most widely read restaurant critic and co-editor of the *Sydney Morning Herald Good Food Guide*. He is the author of *YUM*, a book of stories and recipes.

NORTH INDIAN CURRIES
Pat Chapman Founded the Curry Club in 1982. A regular broadcaster on television and radio, he is the author of 20 books, which have sold more than 1 million copies.

GRILLS AND BARBECUES
Brian Turner Chef/patron of Turner's in Knightsbridge and one of Britain's most popular food broadcasters; he appears frequently on *Ready Steady Cook, Food and Drink* and many other television programmes.

SUMMER AND WINTER CASSEROLES
Anton Edelmann Maître Chef des Cuisines at the Savoy Hotel, London. Author of six cookery books, he has also appeared on television.

TRADITIONAL PUDDINGS
Tessa Bramley Chef/patron of the acclaimed Old Vicarage restaurant in Ridgeway, Derbyshire and author of *The Instinctive Cook*.

DECORATED CAKES
Jane Asher Author of several cookery books and a novel. She has also appeared in her own television series, *Jane Asher's Christmas* (1995).

FAVOURITE CAKES
Mary Berry One of Britain's leading cookery writers, her numerous books include *Mary Berry's Ultimate Cake Book*. She has made many television and radio appearances.

ICE CREAMS AND SEMI FREDDI
Ann and Franco Taruschio Owners of the renowned Walnut Tree Inn near Abergavenny in Wales, soon to appear in a television series, *Franco and Friends: Food from the Walnut Tree*. They have written three books together.

Text © Anne Willan Inc. 1997

Anne Willan has asserted her right to be identified
as the author of this Work.

Photographs © Philip Wilkins 1997

First published in 1997 by
George Weidenfeld & Nicolson
The Orion Publishing Group
Orion House
5 Upper St Martin's Lane
London WC2H 9EA

British Library Cataloguing-in-Publication data
A catalogue record for this book is available from
the British Library

ISBN 0 297 82332 9

Designed by Lucy Holmes
Edited by Maggie Ramsay
Food styling by Louise Pickford
Recipe testing by Justine Wyld
Typesetting by Tiger Typeset